The First Solo Transatlantic Flight

The Story of Charles Lindbergh
and His Airplane, the Spirit of St. Louis

The First Solo Transatlantic Flight

The Story of Charles Lindbergh
and His Airplane, the Spirit of St. Louis

by Richard L. Taylor

Franklin Watts
New York / Chicago / London / Toronto / Sydney
A First Book

Song "Lucky Lindy," words by Wolfe Gilbert and music by Abel Baer. Published by EMI Music Publishers, 810 7th Avenue, New York, N.Y. 10019

Reprinted with permission of Charles Scribner's Sons, an imprint of Macmillan Publishing Company, from THE SPIRIT OF ST. LOUIS by Charles A. Lindbergh. Copyright © 1953 Charles Scribner's Sons, copyright renewed 1981 Anne Morrow Lindbergh.

Cover photographs copyright ©: Tony Stone Images/Lisa Valder; U.S. Air Force Photo (inset)

Photographs copyright ©: Library of Congress: p. 6; Missouri Historical Society: pp. 7, 9, 12, 23 (Erickson), 32, 34 (both Hall), 35 top, 39; Minnesota Historical Society: p. 13; The Smithsonian Institution: pp. 14, 15, 19, 24, 25, 27, 29, 30, 31, 33, 37, 51 top, 54, 55; UPI Bettmann: pp. 17, 48, 52, 60; Museum of Flight, Photographic Collection, Seattle, WA.: p. 20; The Bettmann Archive: pp. 22, 44, 51 bottom; Jay Mallin: pp. 35 bottom, 57; Wide World Photos: pp. 43, 46, 47.

Library of Congress Cataloging-in-Publication Data

Taylor, Richard L.
The first solo transatlantic flight: the story of Charles Lindbergh and his airplane, the Spirit of St. Louis / Richard L. Taylor
p. cm. — (First book)
Includes bibliographical references (p.) and index.
ISBN 0-531-20184-8
1. Lindbergh, Charles A. (Charles Augustus), 1902–1974—Juvenile literature. 2. Air pilots—United States—Biography—Juvenile literature. 3. Spirit of St. Louis (Airplane)—Juvenile literature. 4. Transatlantic flights—Juvenile literature. [1. Lindbergh, Charles A. (Charles Augustus), 1902–1974. 2. Air Pilots. 3. Spirit of St. Louis (Airplane). 4. Transatlantic flights. 5. Aeronautics—History.] I. Title. II. Series.
TL540.L5T38 1995
629.13'0911—dc20   94-27428   CIP
                                                AC

Contents

First Solo Transatlantic Flight

"Lucky Lindy, up in the sky,
fair or windy, he's flying high . . ."

Those are the opening words of a popular song that was written shortly after a twenty-five-year-old pilot named Charles Lindbergh flew from New York to Paris by himself in 1927. To sell newspapers, reporters dreamed up other nicknames, such as the "flying fool" and the "lone eagle." A lot of people thought that Lindbergh was just another daredevil pilot, who one day decided to fly across the ocean to win a prize and hoped his luck would hold out until he reached the other side.

But luck played a small part in Lindbergh's flight, which was the first solo crossing of the Atlantic Ocean.

His success was the result of careful planning, skillful piloting, and an enormous amount of physical and mental endurance.

To get a feeling for what Charles Lindbergh went through, let's pretend that it's 7:30 A.M. on a Friday. You are sitting on a straight-backed wicker chair inside a box with fabric-covered walls. There's not much room. You can touch the sides with your elbows, you can reach the front wall by extending your arm, and your head bumps against the top. There's a small window on each side of the box and one in the roof, but you can't see straight ahead. The chair is not very comfortable because the seat is close to the floor and your legs stretch out in front of you.

You're probably very tired, because you slept only a couple of hours last night, and you had been up all day Thursday. But you have to sit there and stay awake. That's part of the game.

Now it's lunchtime on Saturday, five hours later, and you're still sitting there. Getting sleepy? Arms and legs sore and stiff? Sorry, there's no room to stand up or stretch, and above all, you *must* stay awake.

No matter how badly you want to fall asleep, you've got to sit in that chair all of Friday afternoon and all of Friday night, and you must stay awake until 5:30 P.M.

The interior of the *Spirit of St. Louis* was cramped and uncomfortable. The pilot's seat was chosen for its light weight rather than for comfort.

on Saturday. That's *thirty-three and a half hours* sitting in an uncomfortable chair inside a tiny box. All that time you've talked to no one, you've had only one sandwich and a drink of water, and your ears are ringing from the roar of the big engine with no muffler only a few feet in front of you. By the time the pretending is over, you have been awake for *sixty-three* hours.

Your "chair" is really the pilot's seat of a small airplane named the *Spirit of St. Louis,* and on top of everything else, you've had to keep that airplane under control for thirty-three and a half hours and 3,600 miles (5,794 km). There's no automatic pilot; if you fall asleep you fall into the sea.

The Idea Takes Shape

In 1927, twenty-four years after the world's first flight by Orville Wright, airplanes were still rickety machines made of wood, wire, and fabric. Pilots still sat in open cockpits, engines still quit frequently, and crash landings happened every day. Many people thought that aviation would never amount to anything more than aerobatics and air races. But most pilots believed that airplanes would improve until someday they would carry passengers and cargo all over the world in all kinds of weather.

The first step toward this goal took place in 1926, when the U.S. government arranged to have mail flown between major cities. Airmail was expensive, it wasn't a lot faster than regular mail, and it didn't make a lot of money for the companies that were doing the flying. The Post Office did its best to get the mail delivered on time, even though the old airplanes broke down frequently and bad weather often kept the planes from fly-

Charles A. Lindbergh sits at the controls of his Travel-Air biplane. This photo was taken before the takeoff of Robertson Aviation Corporation's first airmail flight between St. Louis and Chicago, February 20, 1928.

ing. But airmail service began to show people that aviation was no longer a novelty, and that it was becoming more useful and dependable every day.

The Robertson Aviation Corporation of St. Louis, Missouri, was one of those early airmail companies, and Charles Augustus Lindbergh was its chief pilot. Born in Detroit, Michigan, in 1902 and raised in Little Falls, Minnesota, Lindbergh developed an intense interest in machines. He learned to drive a car at age eleven, bought his first motorcycle at sixteen, and dreamed of becoming an airplane pilot.

Lindbergh enrolled as an engineering student at the University of Wisconsin in 1920, but left college after two years. He took a job as a parachute jumper to pay for his flying lessons and finally became a pilot in an air circus. He also spent a full year in flight training to become a U.S. Army aviator. When he was appointed Robertson's chief pilot, Lindbergh had been flying for only four years, but he had much more experience than most pilots his age.

One night in September 1926, Lindbergh was flying toward Chicago in an old biplane with a load of mail. He began to wonder what it would be like if he could just keep on flying. With enough gasoline and a reliable engine, he felt he could "fly on forever through space, past the mail field at Chicago, beyond the state of Illinois, over mountains, over oceans, independent of the world below."

Young Charles Lindbergh and his dog Dingo (left), and as a Second Lieutenant in the U.S. Army Air Corps , March 14, 1925.

A flight like that was a dream, but Lindbergh thought seriously of what he could accomplish with a more efficient airplane. He could carry the mail from St. Louis to Chicago without stopping for fuel. He could save even more time by flying the mail direct to New York. Or he could transport business executives from St. Louis to New York in a fraction of the time it took to get there by train. Lindbergh suddenly realized he might be able to fly all the way across the Atlantic Ocean without stopping.

In September 1926 while flying a biplane such as this Loening, Lindbergh began to consider flying across the Atlantic Ocean.

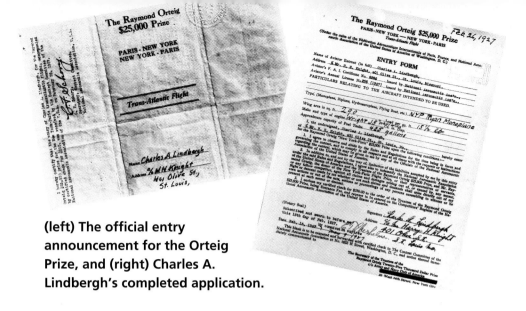

(left) The official entry announcement for the Orteig Prize, and (right) Charles A. Lindbergh's completed application.

In 1926, everyone in aviation was aware of the Orteig Prize, a twenty-five thousand dollar award for the first nonstop flight between New York and Paris. True, the Atlantic Ocean had been crossed by air several times, but only from Newfoundland to Portugal or Ireland, the closest points of land on either side. No one had flown the 3,600 miles (5,794 km) between New York and Paris.

The more he thought about it, the more Lindbergh was sure that he could win the Orteig Prize. He had done everything else he had dreamed about in aviation: he had learned to fly, then he became an army pilot, and now he was the chief pilot of an airmail company. Why couldn't he fly across the ocean? All he needed was an airplane that would carry enough gasoline and an engine that would keep running until he reached Paris.

When he got back to St. Louis, Lindbergh did something that proved he wasn't depending on luck. He wrote down a plan for the trip. His outline included all the things he'd need to do to make the flight a success. The plan would change as he prepared for the flight. But rather than just another pilot who decided one night to fly across the ocean and trust his luck, Charles Lindbergh was in complete control from the very beginning.

Several St. Louis business executives—a banker, a stock broker, the owner of Robertson Aviation Corporation, two newspaper executives, and others— were so impressed with Lindbergh's plan that they formed an organization to finance and manage the trip. Lindbergh added two thousand dollars of his own money to the fund. Because they wanted the world to know of their hometown's interest in the future of aviation, the organization decided to name the airplane the *Spirit of St. Louis.*

Lindbergh poses with several of the financial backers for his solo transatlantic flight.

The Search for an Airplane

An airplane that could carry enough gasoline to fly 3,600 miles (5,794 km) would have to be an airplane that carried little else. To Lindbergh, that meant a single-engine airplane flown by one pilot.

One of the business executives to whom Lindbergh presented his plan suggested that he'd be safer in a plane with several engines so he wouldn't have to land in the water if one of them failed. There were several other aviators making preparations for the transatlantic flight, but none of them had even considered a single-engine airplane.

Lindbergh pointed out that an airplane with two or three engines would be too heavy to stay in the air if one of them quit. Besides, more engines meant more chances of mechanical failure. No, he would rather make the flight by himself, with just one engine.

Before the mid-1920s, there were no airplanes that could have flown 3,600 miles (5,794 km) nonstop, mostly because there were no engines capable of running that long. Then the Wright Aeronautical Corporation introduced a new kind of airplane engine, and it changed everything. The Wright Whirlwind was much lighter and less complicated than other engines, and the builder claimed it would run for nine thousand hours without a failure.

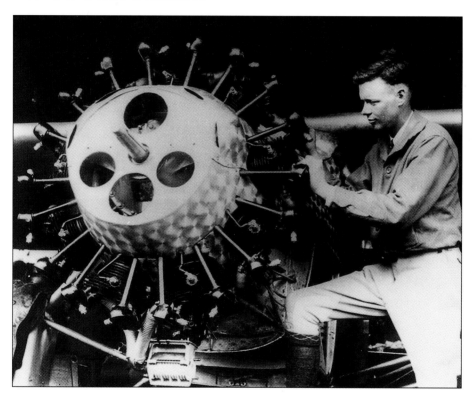

Lindbergh inspects the Wright Whirlwind engine that would power his flight to France. The propeller and spinner have been removed.

This Bellanca WB-2 appealed to Lindbergh because of its fuel capacity and its use of the Wright Whirlwind engine.

One of the new monoplanes (an airplane with one wing instead of two, which is much more efficient) caught Lindbergh's attention. The Bellanca WB-2 had been designed specifically for long-range flights using the new Whirlwind engine. The Bellanca's fuel capacity and the Whirlwind's reliability was the combination Lindbergh needed.

He traveled to New Jersey to see the airplane, only to find out that it had been sold to someone else. He heard of a similar airplane being built by the Travel-Air Company in Kansas, but they refused to sell. They considered a transatlantic flight in a single-engine airplane much too dangerous.

It was now February 1927, and Lindbergh knew

that he had to obtain an airplane very soon, or someone else would win the race. And indeed it was a race; there were five other groups competing for the twenty-five thousand dollar prize.

Lindbergh's list of airplane builders included Ryan Airlines, a small company in San Diego, California, with a reputation for building reliable airplanes. On February 3, Lindbergh sent a telegram to Ryan:

CAN YOU CONSTRUCT WHIRLWIND ENGINE PLANE CAPABLE OF FLYING NONSTOP BETWEEN NEW YORK AND PARIS STOP IF SO PLEASE STATE COST AND DELIVERY DATE

(In 1927 telephoning was so expensive that telegrams—"wires"—were often used instead of long-distance calls. The word *stop* indicated the end of a sentence.)

Ryan Airlines was a young company, eager for business, and they replied by wire the very next day:

CAN BUILD PLANE CAPABLE OF MAKING FLIGHT STOP COST ABOUT SIX THOUSAND DOLLARS WITHOUT MOTOR AND INSTRUMENTS STOP DELIVERY ABOUT THREE MONTHS

After being turned down cold by Bellanca and Travel-Air, Lindbergh was delighted with Ryan's quick response and wired for more information:

COMPETITION MAKES TIME ESSENTIAL STOP
CAN YOU CONSTRUCT PLANE IN LESS THAN THREE
MONTHS STOP PLEASE WIRE GENERAL SPECIFI-
CATIONS

And Ryan did just that. On the afternoon of the
same day, Lindbergh got a wire from San Diego that
gave him the information he needed to go ahead:

GAS CAPACITY THREE HUNDRED EIGHT GALLONS
CRUISING SPEED ONE HUNDRED MILES PER HOUR
STOP CAN COMPLETE IN TWO MONTHS FROM DATE
OF ORDER IF NECESSARY

Enough fuel to make the trip and a cruise speed of
100 miles per hour (161 kph)! Those were better num-
bers than Lindbergh had expected. If Ryan Airlines

**This plane, the Bluebird, drew Lindbergh's
attention to Ryan Airlines. It was the fore-
runner of the *Spirit of St. Louis*.**

RYAN AIRLINES, AIRPLANE MANUFACTORERS, SAN DIEGO, CAL.

The *Spirit of St. Louis* was built in the Ryan Airlines' factory, which formerly was a fish cannery. Only the left portion of the building (where the cars are grouped) was used by Ryan Airlines.

could indeed build the airplane in sixty days, and if it could fly as fast and as far as they had promised, there was still a chance to win the Orteig Prize.

The partners had decided to name their airplane the *Spirit of St. Louis,* and Lindbergh headed west to check on Ryan Airlines. If he liked what he saw, he would stay until the *Spirit* was completed.

Charles Lindbergh arrived in San Diego, California, on February 23, 1927. When he got out of a taxicab in front of the Ryan factory, he wasn't sure he had made the right choice. There were no airplanes in sight, no hangars, not even an airfield. The Ryan factory was located in an abandoned fish cannery on the San Diego waterfront.

B. F. Mahoney, Ryan's young president, and Donald Hall, the chief engineer, welcomed Lindbergh and showed him around the factory. Ryan Airlines was a small business only a few years old, and there were only three airplanes being built. Lindbergh wondered how the company was able to keep going.

The airplanes under construction were called Bluebirds, and they were used to carry passengers on Ryan's small airline between San Diego and Los Angeles. When Mahoney said that his company could build an airplane capable of flying from New York to Paris, he had planned to use the Bluebird design, adding more fuel tanks and making the new airplane larger and stronger.

Lindbergh spent most of that day with Donald Hall. The longer they worked, the more they worked together. Lindbergh told Hall exactly what the *Spirit of St. Louis* would have to do, and Hall made the changes that were needed. At the end of the day, they agreed that the *Spirit* could be built in sixty days, at a cost of $10,580.

**Benjamin Franklin Mahoney,
president of Ryan Airlines and
the builder of the *Spirit of St. Louis***

Lindbergh was very impressed with the people at Ryan Airlines. "They're as anxious to build a plane that will fly to Paris as I am to fly it there," he said. The next day Lindbergh sent a telegram to his partners in St. Louis:

BELIEVE RYAN CAPABLE OF BUILDING PLANE WITH SUFFICIENT PERFORMANCE STOP COST COMPLETE WITH WHIRLWIND ENGINE AND STANDARD INSTRU-MENTS TEN THOUSAND FIVE HUNDRED EIGHTY DOLLARS STOP DELIVERY WITHIN SIXTY DAYS STOP RECOMMEND CLOSING DEAL

Lindbergh's partners sent their approval right away, and on February 25, 1927, the New York-to-Paris project was officially under way.

Donald Hall, chief engineer of Ryan Airlines

The Spirit of St. Louis Takes Shape

Lindbergh needed an airplane that could fly 4,000 miles (6,437 km)—3,600 miles (5,794 km) from New York to Paris, and another 400 miles (644 km) in case he wandered off course or ran into bad weather or strong head winds. That was farther than any airplane had ever flown without stopping, and it would require nearly 400 gallons (1,500 l) of gasoline, far more than the Ryan Bluebird could carry. Major changes would have to be made.

The main body of the airplane (the fuselage) was lengthened by 24 inches (61 cm), and the engine was moved forward 1.5 feet (.46 m) to make room for the larger gasoline tanks. These changes doubled the original Bluebird's weight, and that meant bigger wings to lift the extra pounds. There wasn't time to design an entirely new wing, so Donald Hall simply added 5 feet (1.5 m) to each side. The wheels and shock absorbers were also rebuilt to handle the increased weight.

This model of the Ryan NY-P airplane shows the interior structure of the *Spirit of St. Louis*.

The tail surfaces (the empennage) created a special problem. As an airplane grows, it needs a larger rudder to help the pilot control the left and right movements of the nose. Larger elevators for pitch control of the up-and-down movements of the nose were also necessary. If the tail surfaces are too small, the airplane becomes unstable and tends to move about as it pleases. This makes the airplane very difficult to fly and may even result in the pilot losing control.

Hall knew the *Spirit* should have a larger empennage, but he and Lindbergh decided to use the tail surfaces from the Bluebird. In the first place, there wasn't time to design and build new ones; second, larger surfaces would weigh more; third, Lindbergh was an excellent pilot and knew he could overcome any control problems that might show up.

Keeping the smaller tail surfaces proved to be a life-saving decision. Several times during the transatlantic flight when Lindbergh was so exhausted he couldn't keep his eyes open, the *Spirit of St. Louis* began to spiral down, almost out of control. But as the airplane's speed increased, the noise of the air rushing past the cockpit windows woke him up. He was able to regain control, get back on course, and continue on his way.

Then there was the problem of where to put the pilot's compartment (the cockpit). Hall thought that it should be directly behind the engine, so that the pilot could see everything in front of him. But Lindbergh wanted an enclosed cockpit to protect him from wind and rain, and he didn't care whether he could see to the front—there wouldn't be anyone or anything to watch out for on this flight. Besides, Lindbergh didn't want the big gas tanks behind him. If he had an accident and the *Spirit* hit the ground nose first, he didn't want all that fuel to come crashing down on him.

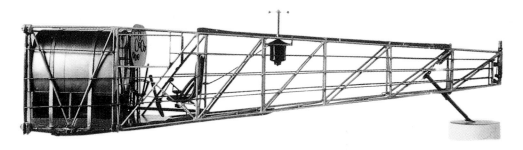

The tail section (above) is the same, smaller one used in the Bluebird. Unlike the wings, which were made of wood, the tail was constructed of welded steel tubing. The simple instrument panel (below) filled the front of the enclosed passenger compartment and contained only those gauges that Lindbergh thought absolutely necessary. Lindbergh's only view was from two small windows in the sides of the cockpit.

So the fuel tanks were installed behind the engine, and the cockpit, completely enclosed in the fuselage, was placed behind the tanks. Small windows on each side of the cockpit provided all the visibility Lindbergh would need for takeoff and landing.

Ryan Airlines' workers put in hundreds of hours of overtime, and three weeks after construction started, the parts and pieces began to look like an airplane. The fuselage and tail surfaces were made of welded steel tubing. To save weight and provide flexibility, the wings were made of wood. Strong beams (spars) ran from wingtip to wingtip, and the spruce ribs that gave the wing its curved shape were placed along the spars every 11 inches (28 cm).

The framework of the *Spirit* was covered with cotton fabric. Workers then brushed on a special paint to stretch the fabric tight and smooth. When it was completed, the entire airplane was painted silver.

The wings of the *Spirit* were made of wood and covered with tightly stretched fabric. This saved on weight and added to the overall flexibility of the wings.

A Ryan worker fills the *Spirit*'s main tank with gasoline.

The Wright Whirlwind engine arrived in early April. It was an internal combustion engine, much like an automobile motor. That is, a mixture of gasoline vapor and air was compressed inside a set of cylinders, then the mixture was ignited at the proper time by spark plugs. As the mixture burned, the increase in pressure forced a piston to move in each cylinder. The pistons were connected to a crankshaft, which turned the propeller, which pulled the airplane through the air.

The Wright Whirlwind was a radial engine, with the nine cylinders arranged in a circular pattern around a central crankshaft. Instead of a heavy water-cooling system, the Whirlwind was cooled by the air flowing around it in flight, making it much lighter and more reliable. It produced more power per pound than any other aircraft engine of its time.

Lindbergh spent nearly all his time at the Ryan factory while the *Spirit* was being built. He supervised every stage of design and construction, making sure that the airplane would be as light as possible. For example, the *Spirit of St. Louis* had no radios, no lights, and no gauges on the fuel tanks.

In addition to supervising the construction of the *Spirit*, Lindbergh worked on navigation charts during his stay at the Ryan factory.

Lindbergh refused to carry a parachute. He even turned down a stamp collector's offer of one thousand dollars just to carry 1 pound (.45 kg) of mail from New York to Paris.

Every ounce of weight he saved meant the airplane could carry that much more fuel, so the *Spirit* became a "flying gas tank." Two large tanks that held 280 gallons (1,060 l) were located between the engine and the cockpit, and three tanks in the wings held 145 gallons (549 l). Lindbergh figured the total of 425 gallons (1,595 l) would be more than enough gasoline to keep the *Spirit* in the air for 4,000 miles (6,437 km).

There was no extra weight in the cockpit, either.

The pilot's wicker seat was chosen not for comfort, but because it was light. The panel directly in front of Lindbergh contained only the instruments that were absolutely necessary: pressure and temperature gauges for the engine, an altimeter, indicators for engine speed and airspeed, a compass, and a turn indicator.

Directly below the instrument panel were the pipes and valves to control the flow of fuel from the tanks to the engine. Gasoline had to be used from the five tanks in the proper order to keep the airplane balanced in flight.

Lindbergh knew there was a chance he'd have to make a forced landing in the ocean, so he made up a survival kit. It consisted of an inflatable rubber raft, four quarts of water, five cans of army rations, a knife, a needle and string, a flashlight, four red flares, a hacksaw blade, and waterproof matches.

This simple wicker chair was certainly uncomfortable for most of Lindbergh's thirty-three-and-a-half-hour flight across the Atlantic.

The wings for the *Spirit* were constructed on the second floor of the Ryan factory. Lindbergh (standing atop the boxcar to the far right) supervises the process. (right) A closeup of the tail section of the *Spirit of St. Louis*.

On April 27, exactly two months from the day Lindbergh and his partners placed the order, the *Spirit of St. Louis* was finished. The registration number "N-X-211" was painted on the wing and tail. ("N" was used on all airplanes registered in the United States, and "X" stood for "experimental.") Instead of a model number, this one-of-a-kind Ryan airplane was called the NYP — "New York-Paris."

Lindbergh Prepares to Fly the Atlantic

After the construction of the *Spirit* was well under way, Charles Lindbergh had time to learn about long-range navigation. Until now, he had used "pilotage"—flying from one town to the next, using whatever landmarks he could see. For most of the transatlantic flight, however, there would be nothing but water in sight. Once beyond the shores of Newfoundland and until he made landfall in Ireland, Lindbergh would have to rely on his magnetic compass. He figured that even if he wandered off course, he surely wouldn't miss the coast of Europe, and he'd certainly be able to recognize something that would guide him on to Paris.

There were no maps for aviators in 1927, but Lindbergh found what he needed at a ship chandler, a store for sailors. He bought maps that covered his route, then cut them into strips that would be easy to handle in the *Spirit*'s tiny cockpit. He drew a line

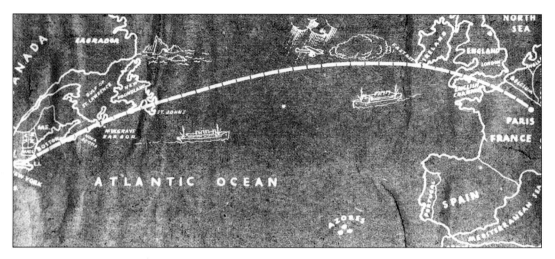

This map traces Lindbergh's journey across the Atlantic to Paris.

from New York to Paris, then marked off thirty-six segments, each one representing approximately one hour of flight. If Lindbergh could stay close to the line he had drawn on the map, he would make it safely across the ocean.

The Spirit Flies for the First Time

Donald Hall, the engineer and designer, had done his work carefully and well. But the *Spirit of St. Louis* was an experimental airplane, and no one really knew how it would fly or how much weight it could carry. The only way to find out was a series of test flights.

On April 28, Lindbergh flew the *Spirit* for the first time at Dutch Flats, the Ryan Company's airfield. The first takeoff was made with very little gasoline in the tanks, and the *Spirit* jumped into the air after a ground roll of only 165 feet (50 m). Lindbergh was delighted with the power and speed of his new airplane. He flew for twenty minutes, checking the controls and instruments. When he landed, he reported to Donald Hall that only a few minor adjustments were needed.

Six days and ten test flights later, Lindbergh and Hall were able to calculate the *Spirit*'s fuel consumption, its airspeed at different power settings, and how far it could fly. This information was converted to

The body of the *Spirit* was towed from the Ryan factory to the Dutch Flats airfield where the final wing assembly would be attached.

charts that would be used to plan the flight across the Atlantic. There was no luck involved here—this was accurate, scientific planning.

Now Lindbergh was ready for the most important test. How much fuel could be put in the tanks without overloading the airplane?

The airfield at Dutch Flats wasn't long enough for

heavy-weight takeoffs, so Lindbergh flew the *Spirit* to Camp Kearney, an abandoned Army post. The old parade ground provided a long, level area with no obstructions. The tests began with only 38 gallons (144 l) of gasoline on board, and Lindbergh planned to continue adding fuel, 50 gallons (189 l) at a time, until he found out how much the airplane could carry safely.

When he got to the 300-gallon (1,140 l) mark, the tires were taking a terrible beating from the loose stones on the field. Knowing that a takeoff or landing accident would probably destroy the airplane and end the project, he decided not to risk the airplane with more tests. Charles Lindbergh and the *Spirit of St. Louis* were as ready as they'd ever be.

The Spirit Heads East

At 3:55 P.M. on May 10, Lindbergh took off from Rockwell Field in San Diego and headed for St. Louis. It would be a fourteen-hour flight and an opportunity to make a thorough check of the *Spirit* and the Whirlwind engine.

By sunset, the *Spirit of St. Louis* was over Arizona, 8,000 feet (2,438 m) above sea level and still climbing to get over the mountains. The course to St. Louis covered some of the most desolate terrain in the United States; there were no cities, no lights, just empty land. With no way to check his position in the dark, Lindbergh flew a heading that he had calculated would keep the wind from drifting the *Spirit* off course, hoping that when the sun rose he'd be able to find his position on the map.

After flying all night, Lindbergh located himself near the town of Parsons, Kansas, only 50 miles (80 km) south of his intended course. He landed at Lambert

Field in St. Louis at 9:20 A.M., fourteen hours and twenty-five minutes from San Diego. It was the fastest anyone had ever traveled from the Pacific coast to St. Louis.

The other pilots in the Orteig race were already in New York, waiting only for a break in the weather over the ocean. Lindbergh knew he had to get to New York as soon as possible if he were to have a chance at winning the race. So after a full night's sleep, he left St. Louis at 8:13 A.M.

Seven hours later, Lindbergh landed at Curtiss Field, near Mineola, New York, where he had arranged for a hangar and mechanics to take care of his airplane. Like most airports in 1927, Curtiss Field was little more than a grassy area where local pilots flew their small airplanes. But only a short distance away was Roosevelt Field. It had a fairly smooth east-west runway—nearly 1 mile (1.6 km) long—enough runway for the *Spirit of St. Louis* to get off the ground with the gasoline tanks filled.

Lindbergh takes off from Rockwell Field in San Diego on his journey East to St. Louis.

Crowds greet Lindbergh and the *Spirit* after the landing of one of several test flights from Curtiss Field.

New York to Paris

By Thursday afternoon, May 19, Lindbergh had been waiting in New York a full week for the weather to improve. There were storms over the Atlantic, fog and rain at Roosevelt Field, and little hope for improvement.

Late that evening, Lindbergh checked once more with the weathermen. There had been a sudden change for the better, and he decided to wait no longer. He would take off for Paris at first light, only a few hours away.

Lindbergh had put in a full day on Thursday, and it was midnight by the time he got to bed, but he couldn't sleep—there were too many thoughts about the long overwater flight running through his mind. After a couple of hours, he got up, dressed, and was driven to Curtiss Field. The ground crew borrowed a truck and towed the *Spirit* up the short road that led to the runway at Roosevelt Field.

A worker pours fuel into the *Spirit of St. Louis* in preparation for Lindbergh's historic flight to Paris.

Now Lindbergh was faced with the most difficult takeoff he had ever attempted. The *Spirit*'s tanks had been filled with 450 gallons (1,690 l) of gasoline, making the airplane heavier than on any of the test flights. The runway was soft and muddy from all the rain, and the wind had shifted so that it was blowing from behind. All of this meant that the *Spirit* would require more distance than ever before to get into the air, and there were telephone wires to climb over at the far end of the runway.

At 7:50 A.M., Lindbergh opened the throttle. The load was so heavy, and the runway was so muddy the *Spirit* barely moved. But with the help of several men pushing on the wing struts, the airplane finally began to gain speed—the flight to Paris was under way.

The halfway mark on the runway flashed by. Lindbergh pulled the control stick backward a bit, and the wheels left the ground. The *Spirit* settled back to the ground several times before it was flying fast enough to stay in the air, but would it clear the wires? In later years, Lindbergh remembered the takeoff:

> The Spirit of St. Louis takes herself off the next time—full flying speed—the controls taut, alive, straining—and still a thousand feet to the web of telephone wires. Now, I have to

After waiting a week for the weather to improve, Lindbergh was finally able to take off from a muddy runway at Roosevelt Field on May 20, 1927.

This aerial shot shows the *Spirit of St. Louis* shortly after takeoff above Long Island farmland.

make it–there's no alternative. It'll be close, but the margin has shifted to my side. I keep the nose down, climbing slowly, each second gaining speed. If the engine can hold out for one more minute—five feet—twenty—forty—wires flash by underneath—*twenty feet to spare*!

When he was 200 feet (61 m) above the ground, Lindbergh leveled off and slowed the engine a bit. The *Spirit* flew solidly at 105 miles per hour (169 kph). At this reduced power setting, there would be more than enough fuel to fly to Paris.

Two hours after takeoff, Lindbergh could see Boston on his left, and Cape Cod on his right. Now he was over the Atlantic, and his next checkpoint was the coast of Nova Scotia, 250 miles (402 km) away over open water.

During the fourth hour of the flight, lack of sleep began to catch up with Lindbergh:

> It would be pleasant to doze off for a few seconds. But I mustn't feel sleepy at this stage of the trip! Why, I'm less than a tenth of the way to Paris; it's not yet noon of the first day. There's still the rest of today and all of tonight, and tomorrow, and part—maybe all—of tomorrow night. After that I can think about being tired, not before. The *Spirit of St.Louis* is doing its job. I've got to do mine. I must stay alert, and match quality of plane and engine with quality of piloting and navigation.

He fought off the urge to take a nap, and suddenly there was Nova Scotia! He crossed the shoreline only 6 miles (10 km) off course. If he did no worse than that across the ocean, he'd be only 50 miles (80 km) off course when he reached Ireland, and he could surely find France—and Paris—from there.

At dusk, almost twelve hours after takeoff, the *Spirit* swooped low over the little city of St. Johns, Newfoundland, the last point on the last island of the North American continent—there was nothing between him and Ireland but the Atlantic Ocean.

All through the night Lindbergh continued eastward, fighting storms and ice and fog. By now he was so tired that he began seeing things and hearing voices, but he forced himself to stay awake.

At last, in the twenty-eighth hour, Lindbergh spotted land ahead of him. The *Spirit of St. Louis* crossed the southwestern coast of Ireland at Dingle Bay, only 3 miles (4.8 km) off course. He was suddenly wide awake, knowing that even if he didn't reach Paris, he had flown the Atlantic Ocean solo without stopping—something that had never been done before.

Lindbergh flew on, across Ireland and the southern tip of England, across the English Channel, and then ... the coast of France and the Seine River, which led directly to Paris.

As Lindbergh recalled later:

With my position known and my compass set, with theair clear and a river to lead me in, nothing but engine failure can keep me now from reaching Paris. The engine is running perfectly—I check the switches again.

The *Spirit of St. Louis* is a wonderful plane. It's like a living creature, gliding along smoothly, happily, as though a suc cessful flight means as much to it as to me, as though we shared our experiences together, each feeling beauty, life, and death as keenly, each dependent on the other's loyalty. *We* have made this flight across the ocean, not *I* or *it*.

I throw my flashlight on the engine instruments. Every needle is in place. For almost thirty-three hours, not one of them has varied from its normal reading. For every minute I've flown there have been more than seven thousand explosions in the cylinders, yet not a single one has missed.

Parisians flocked to Le Bourget Airport in Paris after Lindy's arrival. Headlines in newspapers around the world heralded Lindbergh's accomplishment.

Thirty-three hours and thirty minutes after leaving New York, Charles Lindbergh landed the *Spirit of St. Louis* at Le Bourget Airport in Paris, completing the first solo transatlantic flight. Lindbergh was taken to the American ambassador's home, where he went to bed at 4:15 A.M. Paris time. It had been sixty-three hours since he last slept.

The flight was a tribute to the builders of the *Spirit of St. Louis* and to the perseverance of Charles Lindbergh, whose dream would not be denied.

The morning after Lindbergh landed in Paris, curious people still crowded the airport to look at the machine that had journeyed nonstop across the Atlantic.

After the Flight

When Charles Lindbergh coaxed the *Spirit of St. Louis* from the muddy runway at Roosevelt Field, he had only one objective—fly this airplane to Paris without stopping. He had no plans beyond that, but during the long night over the Atlantic, he thought about how he would get home. Maybe he could continue eastward and fly the rest of the way around the world. That would mean a lot of stops, but such a flight would set new records for distance and speed, and it would certainly get everyone's attention. It would show that airplanes could fly anywhere on the face of the earth.

But he didn't realize how much attention his transatlantic flight had already attracted. Not only had he won the twenty-five thousand dollar prize, Lindbergh had been promoted to the rank of colonel in the U.S. Army and had become a hero overnight.

The American people weren't ready to share Lindbergh with the rest of the world until they had a chance to give him the honors he deserved. President Coolidge solved the problem when he sent a navy cruiser, the USS *Memphis,* to bring Lindbergh back to the United States. So Lindbergh flew the *Spirit* from Paris to Gosport, England, where the airplane was dismantled and placed aboard the ship for the journey home.

When the *Memphis* steamed into New York Harbor, a huge crowd was on hand. Several days later, 4.5 million people lined the streets of Manhattan for the official welcoming parade. "Colonel Lindbergh," said the mayor, "the city of New York is yours." And the rest of the world was his as well; overnight, Lindbergh became the most admired man of his time.

More than five hundred vessels jammed New York Harbor to welcome Charles Lindbergh back from Paris. Approximately three hundred thousand people filled the southern tip of Manhattan to greet the returning hero.

Lindbergh's ticker tape parade drew 4.5 million people into the streets of Manhattan. Charles A. Lindbergh was the most famous and admired man in the world.

From the very beginning, Lindbergh wanted his flight to make people aware of what airplanes could do. He realized that he had a wonderful opportunity to carry aviation's message to the entire country. So the *Spirit* was put back together and on July 20, Lindbergh started on a nationwide tour. In the following ninety days, he flew over nearly every state and landed in eighty-two cities to give the people a close look at the first airplane to fly nonstop from New York to Paris. He demonstrated the *Spirit*'s reliability (and showed that his flight across the Atlantic was not just a lucky adventure!) by flying nonstop from Washington, D.C., to Mexico City, a trip that took twenty-seven hours and fifteen minutes.

In the years that followed, Lindbergh saw his dreams come true as airlines developed rapidly all over the world. His transatlantic flight was the spark that started this growth, and he continued as an adviser to the aviation industry for many years. More than any other individual, he showed the world that air travel could be comfortable, safe, and efficient.

The *Spirit of St. Louis* was designed and built to do just one thing—to fly from New York to Paris—and the Ryan company never built another airplane like it. Lindbergh felt that the *Spirit* should be preserved, so when his goodwill tour came to an end, he donated the airplane to the Smithsonian Institution, keeper of our nation's treasures. Today, the *Spirit of St. Louis* is displayed in the National Air and Space Museum in Washington, D.C., where it hangs—as if still in flight—in a gallery with the Wright Flyer, the Bell X-1, and other aircraft that represent "firsts" in aviation.

Often when his travels brought him to Washington, D.C., Charles Lindbergh visited the aviation museum of the Smithsonian. Unrecognized, he would stand in the shadows and gaze at the *Spirit of St. Louis*, the little silver airplane that had carried him from New York to Paris and into aviation history.

Charles Lindbergh died at his home on the island of Maui on August 26, 1974.

Today, the *Spirit of St. Louis* hangs in a place of honor in the nation's capital at the National Air and Space Museum of the Smithsonian Institution.

Facts and Figures

The Spirit of St. Louis
Ryan Model NYP ("New York-Paris")

Dimensions

Wingspan	46 feet (14 m)
Length	27 feet 8 inches (8.4 m)
Height	9 feet 10 inches (3.0 m)
Fuel capacity	450 gallons (1,690 l)
Oil capacity	25 gallons (95 l)

Weight (At takeoff from Roosevelt Field)

Empty weight	2,150 pounds (975 kg)
Pilot	170 pounds (77 kg)
Miscellaneous	40 pounds (18 kg)
Fuel	450 gallons (1,690 l)
	2,750 pounds (1,247 kg)
Oil	20 gallons (95 l)
	140 pounds (64 kg)
Total weight	5,250 pounds (2,381 kg)

Performance

Maximum airspeed	119.5 mph (192.3 kph)
Minimum (stall) airspeed	72 mph (116 kph)
Range (zero wind)	4,210 miles (6,775 km)
Takeoff distance	2,500 feet (762 m)

Engine — Wright Whirlwind J-5C

Power at sea level	220 horsepower
Normal operating speed	1,800 RPM
Displacement	788 cubic inches (12.9 l)
Compression ration	5.2
Weight (no oil)	500 pounds (227 kg)
Fuel consumption, at 200HP	17.7 gallons/hour (67.0 l/h)

Total flying time when delivered to the Smithsonian Institution (Only two other pilots flew the *Spirit,* 10 minutes each)	489 hours 28 minutes
Total number of flights	174
Flying time, New York to Paris	33 hours 30 minutes 29.8 seconds

U.S. President Calvin Coolidge awards a medal to Lindbergh in honor of his historic accomplishment.

For Further Reading

Boyne, Walter J. *The Smithsonian Book of Flight for Young People.* New York: Atheneum, 1988.

Burleigh, Robert. *Flight: The Journey of Charles Lindbergh.* New York: Philomel Books, 1991.

Collins, David R. *Charles Lindbergh, Hero Pilot.* New York: Chelsea House, 1991.

Rosenblum, Richard. *Aviators.* New York: Facts on File, 1992.

————. *Wings, the Early Years of Aviation.* New York: Four Winds Press, 1980.

Visual Dictionary of Flight. New York: Dorling Kindersley, 1992.

Williams, Brian and Francis Phillipps. *Pioneers of Flight: Tales of Courage.* Austin, Tex.: Steck-Vaughn, 1990.

Index

About the Author

Richard L. Taylor is an associate professor emeritus in the Department of Aviation at Ohio State University, having retired in 1988 after twenty-two years as an aviation educator. At retirement, he was the Director of Flight Operations and Training, with responsibility for all flight training and university air transportation. He holds two degrees from Ohio State University: a B.S. in agriculture and an M.A. in journalism.

His first aviation book, *Instrument Flying*, was published in 1972, and continues in its third edition as one of the best-sellers in popular aviation literature. Since then, he has written five more books for pilots, and hundreds of articles and columns for aviation magazines.

Taylor began his aviation career in 1955 when he entered U.S. Air Force pilot training, and after four years on active duty continued his military activity as a reservist until retirement as a major and command pilot in 1979.

Still active as a pilot and accident investigator, as well as a writer, Taylor flies frequently for business and pleasure. His books for Franklin Watts include *First Flight*, *The First Solo Flight Around the World*, *The First Flight Across the United States*, and *The First Supersonic Flight*, *The First Human-Powered Flight*, and *The First Transcontinental Air Service*. He and his wife Nancy live in Dublin, a suburb of Columbus, Ohio.